SOMEWHERE BETWEEN

Carol Fortino

Somewhere Between
© 2017, Carol Fortino

No part of this book may be reproduced by any means known at this time or derived henceforth without written permission of the publisher or author. The exception would be in the case of brief quotations embodied in the critical articles or reviews and pages where permission is specifically granted by the publisher or author.

Books may be purchased in quantity and/or special sales by contacting the publisher. All inquiries related to such matters should be addressed to:

Middle Creek Publishing & Audio
9027 Cascade Avenue
Beulah, CO 81023
editor@middlecreekpublishing.com
(719) 369-9050

Cover Image: "Somewhere Between" by Ted Fusby
Cover Design: David A. Martin, Middle Creek Publishing
Printed in the United States

First Edition, 2017

ISBN: 978-0-9989322-8-6

For my daughter

Alia Bergeven Morgan
October 24, 1971 – October 15, 2017

SOMEWHERE BETWEEN

Carol Fortino

<u>Middle Creek Publishing & Audio</u>
Beulah, CO • USA

Contents

Beginnings

Credo	3
Flaneur	4
Architexturing	6
Westcliffe Hike	8
Mountain Trailing	9
Hawaiian Bridesmaid	10
Oxfordian Economy	12
Weekend	15
The First Second Encounter	16
Triadamen	17
Leaps of Faith	18
Beaucoup de Gens Differente	19
An Interim Friendship	20
Pottery and Warm Cider	22

Somewhere Between

Somewhere Between	27
St. Ives Golf Resort	28
Waiting	30
The Sameness of Being	31
Linz	32
The Inexorable Wheel	33
Glasshouse Five	34
Bookmark	35
Full Disclosure	36
Mother's Day	38
Again	39
Quantum	40

Resolutions

Bridges	45
Lost Books	46
Hot Winds Blown Dry	47
Marriage Flight	48
On the Pier of No Return	49
Goethe on the Titanic	50
Savages Road	51
Sharawadji, Graceful Disorder	52
Bittersweet Resolve	53
The Shadow of Yeti	54
She Didn't Come	55
Figure in the Landscape	56
The Farm at Blende	58
Live Exhibition	59
Enlightened Dignity	60
Eleventh Hour World	61
Spyglass	62
The Journey's End	64

These poems are about relationships - their tenuous beginnings, their mid-points -somewhere in between, their resolutions or ending. Some words are loving, mystifying, sad, uncontrollable, and even a bit sarcastic or funny. These are emotions that run the gamut of relationships. May you find one that especially speaks to you.

Beginnings

Credo

Humans are electro-bio-chemical
learning machines
Housed in a thin-skinned sack
Liquids sloshing about.

But humans can investigate
heredity
To comprehend their internal environment.

They can pursue
knowledge
to modify their external environment.

If coupled with the obligation
of self-control,
Humans can attempt to lead
their best possible life.

Flâneur

He strolls the city without destination.
An observer, *désengagé*
From the crush of human flow
Experiencing the constructs of his fellow man.
Street layouts, buildings, window frames
Flower-boxes, peeling paint, rusty doorknobs.
Details one can't take in fully
On a rushing bike or bus or car.

Have you ever been a *flâneur*
A stroller, a dawdler
Loitering in a foreign neighborhood
Absorbing the nuances
As Baudelaire would have you be?

New lovers kissing on the street corner.
Modishly styled and coiffed
Embracing in a seductive way.

The old French couple holding hands,
The beautiful octogenarian with her elegant scarf,
Strolling in a loving way.

The arguing couple shouting as they walk off
Their overcoats flapping like their hands
Hoping in a tentative way.

Have you ever been a *flâneur*
A stroller, a dawdler
Loitering in a foreign neighborhood
Absorbing the nuances
As Baudelaire would have you be?

Architexturing

Love is like a fine architectural drawing
Broad-brush strokes
Delineate a general outline.
But even then, you can tell
If it's a design worth following.

It will be the small refinements that turn
This print into a work of art.
Even erasures are necessary
To blur or clarify a point, as needed.

Learning to love is like
Tracing a blue line on a white print
Knowing each corner
Sensing each curve.

First-time technique
Is over-rated, under-pleasured
Broad brush-strokes of promise.

There is an excited challenge
When bodies learn to blend to subtle lines
Tracing a sensation
Imprinting a style.

Next-time love experiments, fulfills
Slowly a structure evolves
From fine lines to prospective depths.

Massage
Masseuse
Masseur
Messenger, message.

Rated-over pleasure
Under architecturing.

Westcliff Hike

One tiny seed in a parachute pod
Wafting in the mountain air
Sinking on the dying wind
Caught in the branch of a fallen tree.

Silvery arms radiate toward the sun.
Twirling down to the earthly brown
Absorbing rich nutrients
Waiting to germinate in early spring.

Nature's miracle on an autumn breeze.

Mountain Trailing

I should not have thought of you
In this granduress scenery
And tent-side beanery.

My mind should be open
To echoing bird calls
And be flower enthralled.

Yet in my lowing consciousness streams
a memory
into words
onto touch.

Does that momentary intimacy
Close off the blossoming
Of possible loveship?

Like the thigmotropism of vine on limb
closing round
by gentle touch.
Symbiotic, not parasitic
A Venus fly-trap,
A nocturnal Four O'Clock
Unfolded in starlight.

NO! This friendship is a moonrise,
A sunslippery dawn.

Hawaiian Bridesmaid

Sayde got back from the hair braiding
With the bridesmaids and bride to be.
Her peach gown hung on the bedroom rack
Hibiscus designs in the weave.

Jeff came in and sat on the old couch
"The wedding is not until three
Let's go surf and we'll be back by one.
It will only be you and me."

"My wildish hair is already fixed
And I don't want to it to come free.
Beside the surf's running low right now
With waves not much higher than three."

"Let's do it anyway," said her beau
Tugging her gently off the seat
"Ok," she said, "but we can't be long
Especially in mid-morning heat."

They loaded their fiberglass surfboards
And drove to their favorite beach
Running toward the surging ocean
Across the sand, skipping their feet.

Into the water, feeling the swell
Paddling strongly against the sea
Watching the azure wave climb upward
A slight chill from the Pacific breeze.

On her board Sayde turned for the break
It curled around her taut body
Whispering water washed through her braids
Champagne bubbles made her giddy.

Coming back to their local pad
Sayde slipped on her Hawaiian gown
Peach tones set off her deep tan.
And they rushed to the wedding in town.

Oxfordian Economy

Rich friends can coax you
To do outlandish things!

A night at the Oxford Hotel
A four-poster bed with canopy of blue
Tall armoire on plush, dark carpet
Renovated to its state of glory
Like the resurrection possible
In this night.

All my usual friends were busy
Leaving me no accustomed shelter.
I had only planned on Motel Six or maybe even Eight.
While I counted pennies in my head.
 Figuring the travel reimbursement
Dividing by two.

Whence had I become so miserly?
He reminds me that my father is rich,
But I counter that the child is not the father.
While this man's inheritance has been guaranteed
From generation to generation
Mine is of a grandfather working hard and
A father absent to make his mark.

We made do -
Finding sales and bringing back the change.
It all paid off in the end, in some ways.
But the newly rich never take wealth for granted.

The hardened calluses are too thinly camouflaged
Under skin just recently softened.
The sweat of labor is too near the night-sweats,
And age too far gone to fight with the tenacity of youth.

I sensed a cavalier attitude in the rich man's child,
Knowing in the end his wealth is guaranteed
That he will control at least as much
As his father, or more.

My own children have echoes of false hope
Presuming certain gifts and privileges.
But unbeknownst, they are caught betwixt,
No touchstone of imprinted wealth,
Left only with a mere allusion of labor's receipt.
There is a selfishness amidst the new opulence.

But why not enjoy this night of splendor
With its triple-sheeted bed and
Body-deep porcelain tub,
Fireplace with fresh flowers on the mantle
And the vertical lift that raised me to this level?

When he leaves, I will enclose myself
Within the darkness and wait
For the complimentary morning wake-up call.
We will go out for a sumptuous brunch
at the Brown Palace
For which he will kindly pay.

Then I can mentally divide the cost and
Factor it into to my modest travel allowance
Wondering to myself
If I am just a hapless relic, like this Victorian décor
Or caught in a rich friend's hoax.

Weekend

From sun to peaceful snow
Vigorous hills to quiet fireglow
We had such different perspectives
Of the weekend.

Shirt-sleeve weather, hike to the top
Rock climbing and view-time stops
From the equilateral tree of peace
We took karmic energy.

Indolently we lie abed
Few times like this are ahead
Taking off a day from pressure.
Tomorrow we will work.

Silent snow induces study time
I feel your unsettled rhyme
Our unconscious expectations
Are widely different.

Cabin layback is what I need
On that my spirit sorely feeds
Other pleasures are possible
But not required.

My sensations sift clear and fine.
Yours walk a bleaker line
Perhaps we can fuse our views
To pleasant memories.

The First Second Encounter

You sense the need
For affirmation of my womanhood.
A slightly more aggressive male
To move and remove
Any lingering self-doubt
To leave me receptive
To a new gentle friendship.

Triadamen

Three men impinge
Upon the blankness of my soul
A gay friend
A penniless philosopher
A married lover.

Each bringing a dimension
That colors the flavor
Of my quarks
Artistic expression
Ethereal thought
Salty earth.

And then, another?

Leaps of Faith

Coincidences in life
Sometime take us to places
We never dreamed.

Business meetings, casual acquaintances
Social interaction, open to chance
Infatuation leading to love, marriage.

Remarriage, renewed chances
Hope, once again
Leaps of Faith.

Beaucoup de Gens Differente

Photographs of the Toykyo café
Admidst high-tech buildings of glass and steel.
Inside strangers sitting alone, not conversing
Intending to become invisible in the crowd.

Survival depends on anonymity.

Photographs of the Stompin' Grounds cafe
Admist local buildings sheltered by pines
Inside strangers and friends say hello.
Signals that you belong.

Survival depends on community.

In Beulah you can be a hermit or an extrovert.
In Japan you can be an extrovert or a hermit -
Both on the same day.

An Interim Friendship

Skittish children, watching, reacting
Small town parade, twirlers marching
Lasagna and apple pie in a church basement.

A Bishop's Castle architect
Climbing a wholly, holey rock
Blazing yellow of aspen.

How did we get here figuratively,
Mentally – a bathtub physics conversation.
Eating Mexican food, or digesting jazz.
Our mutual friend lent the cabin.
A fateful kindness,
a need.

Playing tennis at twilight
Racing an exuberant track.
Money lost in a sock
Counting satellites and shooting stars
Watching the Perseus
shower of warmth.
With three kids on a blanket.

We bought. boots at the garage sale
Shared warmth of coffee and rolls
Quiet conversation, revealing thoughts
A quiet touch of friendship, a new warming sweater
Hiking the hills, leaving invited guests behind
But glad you stayed
To look at the Smurf Village in the valley.

Flowing towards Florissant
Sharing my favorite place
Bright sun and blue hues
Secrets
of the Nature Place.
Inner peace at the Interbarn
Acknowledging
you to friends.

Cripple Creek in late afternoon
A miniature set of bathtub regalia.
Your thesis partly read, but well understood.
A dare, an affair revealed
No scorn, an understanding, sharing
Maybe even future caring for where
A singed soul must passage.

It's unusual being compared to
A complex carbohydrate
"It's either you or the sugar"
Music sung on a full moon ride.

To the spare man in the attic?
Is the man in the attic spare
To build an igloo?
With only a frost-bitten Californian design.
White knuckles riding on ice - Riunite
A cautious kiss overlooking
Frosted silhouettes at night, so nice.

Time's passing, closing to goodbye
Pastels on mylar skylines

Pottery and Warm Cider

A frost smoke of breath
A touch of class,
Coor's slopper
A farewell and thoughts of Hawaiian dreams
Shared melancholia
A trombe wall, built for warmth, remembrance
An environmental curtain,
Drawn agilely thought a curvilinear friendship.

Somewhere Between

Somewhere Between

Somewhere between the dutiful and the dull,
The dreamer's gossamer drapery
Must be a midpoint-
A love for all seasons.

One which cannot sway
Above the pendulum's ethereal arc
Waiting potentially,
To sweep into kinetic motion.

One which cannot sink
Lower than the dutifully suspended link
Drawing in the sands
Deliberate Foucaultian designs.

Love that gracefully oscillates
Somewhere between the original plane of motion,
Tracing ever-changing patterns
For the remaining seasons of our lives.

St. Ives Golf Resort

A fashion-challenged man,
belly protruding over a belt holding up
his blue-striped Bermuda golf shorts
sits with his wife, a slightly-aged vixen
with blonde hair, smiling pleasantly.

She, in her salmon, three-quarter sleeve top
with white linen Capri pants
nods to the other women around the birthday table.
They push back chairs and get up to dance
leaving grey-haired men sitting stoically.

The young woman singer from the band
"Honesty and the Liars"
smiles at the dancing matrons'
swinging arms and swaying hips.
then joins them in the freestyle circle with her mike.

When the raucous song ends,
an older woman stops by the table
of a middle-aged lady sitting alone,
tapping her feet, sipping her glass of wine.

"I can tell that you like to dance,
so next time move your bod and join us."
And so she did encouraged by the blunt invitation.
The dance floor is crowded for "Ride Around Sally"
Young and old dancing their style from the 60s to 90s.

The guitarist takes a puff on his e-cig
and stuffs it in his back pocket
without missing his riff.
but the annoying smell wafts across
the no-smoking room.

Only one trophy wife in the room,
thin, jet black hair to match her long silk dress.
a short-cropped golden sweater is set off
with a multi-layered shiny necklace.
Her partner smiles, old and patient.

Golf buddy camaraderie shared by wives -
friends of many years.
And young men in from the greens
 on a date-night without the kids.

Money well-tamed thought the single lady
A nice welcome to St. Ives Michigan Golf Resort.

Waiting

You never took the time to ask
How do I feel?
No love expressed, waiting for the turning point.
I hold back, waiting
Making sure that you feel appreciated.
Finally, I ask, do you wonder how I feel?

Stymied by tardy waiting;
Plateaued with indecisive waiting;
Exonerated by no more waiting.

Waiting for what?

The Sameness of Being
(inspired by Eckhart Tolle, A New Earth, 2005)

Before you, before me
Before him, before her
Can I find my true self?
Or has my ID been hidden
Changed, manipulated by
Friends
Family
Children
Lovers
Peers
Students
Salespeople
Pets
Cosmos

Who, what am I?
Does my EGO seek superiority or balance
Between me and the SUPEREGO of our times?

I am just trying to live in alignment at 70 plus years
With the sameness of being.

Linz

That day
which I spent with you
Is abstracted
from the myriad flow of time.
Hours not to be forgotten
to be remembered.

Fog,
hovering over river, house
and clinging window,
crept inside my mind
pressing me into the vortex
of your talking arms.

We danced, foreign
music played. To me, the stranger
words were mere diversion
from your purpose
not undermined by self-turned fear.

A dancing body exited
from the door
Where the mind, like fog, awaited
reassuring sun of consciousness,
But skeletal memory feared
the return to flesh.

The Inexorable Wheel

When you climb up
The round circle of fate
And reach the final apex
You must decide if you'll ride.

Or hesitating,
Life will spin you down
And like old Sisyphus
You must work your way up again.

Each spoke he puts in place
Makes the wheel more sound
Wooden spikes in iron rims
Keep you turning endlessly.

The rutted road will try
To dislodge the progress you make.
Unless you decide to jump off at the cycle's top,
You're doomed to spiral down once more
Into codependency.

Glasshouse Five

We had to get directions from a bronze-chested lad,
His stubby shorts were barely covered
by denim chaps.
"Of course, I noticed him," she sent up her
Australian companion,
"But I spared him my American charm".

So we drove to the observatory
To see the volcanic dikes standing proudly separate,
Subterranean hand-holding in the morning shine
Keeping their distance in this erosional landscape.

Igneomatic fire once melted the heart chambers
Pressuring the magma by twists of fate
Forming stark geologic sentinels
Now pared down from their youthful stance.

Volcanic energy forged dissimilar minerals
Like those in this relationship, not yet lithified
But chiseled finely by daily contact.
Friends can only observe the diurnal posturing
Of the mysterious glass-house five.

Bookmark

It is as if I were a bookmark,
Place-holding the latest
Chapters of your life's novel
Betwix work and retirement.

Chapters of adventure,
Hiking, kayaking, and canoeing
Essays on travel,
Italy, Germany, New Orleans retold.

Time means little to you.
Pick up your autobiography at will.
Let it wait,
No haste.

There comes a turning point
When you decide to start
Engaging again.

The bookmark, attractive and colorful,
Is laid aside
Without much thought
While you turn to new pages.

Full Disclosure

Of late, he is smitten with a woman
quite recently met.
As someone who looks both ways
Before crossing the street,
Emotionally speaking, this surprised him.

He wrote:
You are on the Eyes-Only-Need to Know list
For the full disclosure of my intentions.
If he was vague, it was not to deceive.

His sleep was difficult last night thinking
He had with vagueness caused me pain.
No need to cause considerable damage
To the self-image of an honest man.

But, for a moment I thought I was loved.
Sorry I misunderstood.

I replied:
There were no firm ties between us.
In our sporadic, long-distance romance.
I still value you for your intellect
and adventurous spirit.

We asked:
Can we continue walks in the woods, dinners, stars and books?
Because loving friends are hard to find
and we are good ones.

Mother's Day

Vigilance is kept
In the sea
Gray and dark.

The meter of sunlight squeezes
a military tempo.
Portside days are marked
by metronomic waiting.
Your sub will play basso sotto
in the cacophony of war.

Departure is imminent.
The gray sea deepens.

I hear
Rhythm from the topside mates.
Rhythm of the sun-splashed waves.
Rhythm of a child's da-dee dah.

A whistle blows, a line is thrown.
The rising crescendo fades.
Silent tears circle outward
Into the deep gray sea of my heart.

Again

He didn't come to the cabin today
Did he feel that he'd be in the way?
The job he scheduled suddenly
Was probably a ruse to get free.

No meeting of two friends again.

Not that either wanted to meet.
They're both alarmingly discreet
About not saying a word
Of the other that they've heard.

I could keep their mention separate again.

And yet I'd like my lover to meet
To know my friend and discover
That each has a special part of me
That the other doesn't acknowledge.

With them both I am complete again.

Quantum

"Streams have more than one response to rocks."
Around, under, back-up eddy currents,
Over and beyond.
Chaotic movements leading to "order-
These brief moments seized from disorder."
Evolving into newer, higher forms-
Streams, lakes, rivers, oceans.

Women have more than one response to men.
Around, under, back-up family currents,
Over and beyond
Chaotic choices leading
to order.
Those brief years seized from disorder
Evolving into newer, more complex relationships
Where we give up predictability for potential.

Yet neither streams nor people
Exist independently of relationships.
Rocks, meanders, slopes, and hills
Evoke different responses from streams.

Friendship, love, addiction, abdication
Evoke different responses from women.

Influence on behavior
is not
Found in polar opposites.
Right or left,
love or hate.

The quantum world says, "It depends."
On relationships created momentarily
Between streams and obstacles,
Between men and women
With quantum leaps of complimentarity
Yet uncertainty.

Human love, like a stream, is not one thing.
It is a relationship, playing
Amidst "vast networks of interference patterns."
Celebrated within a "continuous dance of energy."

Resolutions

Bridges

Keep the walkway open
From the old year to the new
Even if sad memories haunt
Your present gratitude.

Unlike the long and rickety bridge.
Life has but a narrow span,
Cross the turbulent waters now
While familial ties still stand.

Lost Books

What books are lent to a lover?
And how do you get them back,
Or do you want them
Or they need you?

"Openings" a Bob Samples philosophy
Of love and life, like our beginnings
But now mutually, purposefully closed down.

"Blackberry Summer" a Margaret Mead adventure
Rather like our own
Opportunities taken at a whim, enjoyed, remembered.

"Milagro Beanfield War"
We didn't understand the implications of that title.
Subtle biases in a relationship
Partially alluded to, inadvertently acted out.

Maybe we should meet someday- later-
And exchange our piles of books
Catch up over coffee.
See if "The Conquest of Land" or "Seven Nations"
Still mean the same.

Maybe you can't have the same conversation twice.
Maybe some books are just not yours anymore.

Hot Winds Blown Dry

Relationships can parch
The poetry from your soul
Like the rattling of dry gourds
Blowing down a narrow arroyo.

What seems like friendship
Is frenetic activity,
Scuttling of a kangaroo rat
Searching seeds in a déserted skull.

Shaded moments in the arms of a saguaro
Are mistaken for respite,
As persistent sun desiccates the bond
Crackling it like dry rawhide.

Marriage Flight

Someday when he
has found his keel,
I'll be able to race the wind
and chase a dream.
Knowing I have
the freedom to fail.

And if this never
comes to pass
Like a gull, I'll have to fly
away hoping
His skiff won't upheave
leaving a soul-mate to die.

For if he can sail alone,
(and I pray he can)
The strength of freedom
will have unbound us both.

On the Pier of No Return

Sunset at Heron Island
At last, the last time
No romancing the stone here!

Does the frigate bird
Perched on the sign post
Know that I am just one more girlfriend
Brought here one more time?

Sign posts all along the way
Just a last hurrah for love.
No mating for life.

Goethe on the Titanic

As the warning bells rang out
and the band played on,
The old gentleman remembered
his school day's Goethe.

"Life belongs to the living
And he who lives
Must be prepared for change".
Frightened, he pondered.

Did I eat my dessert?
If I am I circling the drain,
did I do it right
for my wife, for my life?

Did my wife unloosen
her whalebone corset
As she dropped
into the lifeboat?

Savages Road

Wild lantana strangling the rainforest growth
Forcing its way up leafy hills
And down flooded bush country creeks.

The tangled vines reflect my inner countenance,
While living on Savages Road.

I came with such love and promise
Joyous runs past mailboxes unique
Showing pride in Queenslanders' homes.

I left with an aching lost for neighbors and friends
Walking with sadness untold.

No love in the house on Savages Road
No giving of gifts, cold indifference
No material gain, only spiritual pain
A promise never unfolded.

A house with deceit is a savage place.
It can never become a home.
The philanderer of hope and companionship
Will find himself - old, arthritic and alone.

Sharawadji, Graceful Disorder

My life is frozen in graceful disorder
Like the quartz molecules
Of my bedroom window pane.

I have been like the little black and golden Whistler
Who flies at the window
In the early streaks of dawn
Attacking its own reflection
Veering off at angles,
Self-flagellating its image, ungracefully.

Only when the angle of the sun rises,
Does the mirage of an imaginary attacker fade.
The bird regains its sense of order
And flies away.
Is it time for me to also rise and fly away
Before "Sharawadji" becomes entropy
And my glass façade shatters?

Bittersweet Resolve

Caring,
Leads to depression
If one allows too much sway
Over her emotions.
Yet, not caring,
Leads to indifference
And survival of the witless.

And so,
You will miss me
In this life before death
For all the possible moments
And the loss of our continuity.

The Shadow of Yeti

He ran through the forest
Flames licking behind him,
Around, up, over and through
Until he fell down, subdued.

Dethroned like modern man
Crackling sounds as branches flashed.
Couldn't hold their crowns anew.
Ancient wisdom slain - Yeti knew.

Pride kept us from thinning our forests
We knew better than nature, of course
Wire on wire sparked tongues of fire
For trees and brush historically fueled.
The forest cries with barren voice
Thin trunks shadow the slopes
The ash is buried beneath the snow
Winter sun can't break the dew.

Spring will unleash torrents of rain
Flood water will wash into creeks
Homes, cars and roads will run amok
Yet skies will be sunny and blue.

We must heed the advice of Yeti
To care for our forest and land
Because careless or nature-born fire
Will ravish humans anew.

She Didn't Come

Waiting at the Paris train station
Bouquet in my hand
Anxious to see her again.

The train is on time.
Passengers file up the escalator.
I watch expectantly.

I place the flowers in the rubbish bin
Hands-free to call her cell
No response only voicemail.

Elle n'est pas venue.

Figure in the Landscape

What can one see this cloudy day
Waiting for my night flight back home?
A chance walk in Auckland's new park -
A tall statue catches my eye.

Face on
Fingers wrap around her torso
Gently caressing well-formed breasts
Not from ego as it might seem
But from compassionate self-love.

Head on
Her face is not a stone figure
But a rose ready to blossom
Plant and human intertwining
A statue broadening my mind.

Side on
Her fingertips merge together
Lengthening from the slender arms
Wrapping from shoulder to buttocks
Accentuating sturdy legs.

Back on
Her hand and thumb become leaves
A vine circling her sculpted back
Entwining round a twisting spine
Anchored by her amorphous feet.

A moment's pause to contemplate
The message of the bronze statue.
Can a woman morph to new forms.
Or is she bound by old conventions?

The Farm at Blende

Emanating echoes
From the silent ground.
Men move on
To empty fruits of their labor.

The harvest completed
Plenty reaped once more.
Women wait
To resurrect fertile dreams.

Live Exhibition

The white moon
Solitary
I live myth
Alone.
My quest for escape.

Enlightened Dignity

I regret that I must inform you
A friendship of any sort is not possible.
This is predicated by my own peculiarities,
Self-interest and motivation.
I can't give a satisfactory explanation
For this sudden decision of mine.
I know you will have the enlightened dignity
To respect my feelings and protect your own.

Eleventh Hour World

Do I understand the zeitgiest of my time
While I create a personal path toward eternity?
Will it be the right ending for my life?

Not from stupidity nor morbidity
Do I seek an affinity for the now
And clarity for the moment that I die.

Some will claim that my childhood religious beliefs
Ebbed away at the university in Berkeley.
But that is not the case.

High school eroded my dogmatic stance,
Of the literal ecclesiastical words of the Nicene Creed
That I could no longer recite, in good faith.

Self-study and time honed a spirituality,
With hope in an afterlife and after-being
of some unfathomable kind.

And so my epitaph might read
As scattered ashes waft
From Colorado mountain top and California seashore.

"She was an eclectic, pragmatic, humanist
Trying to live a worthwhile life as best she could."

Spyglass

I wish I could believe in a personal god
As I did as a child and into a seeking adulthood.
But the phantasm disappeared with biblical complications,
Historical facts and continuing skeptical science.

The faith of Thomas Merton inspired me to look again.
But night sky confirmed my doubt, yet left me hope.
Is there an intelligence spying at the wars and squabbles
On this earthly orb, infinitesimal in the universe?

What hubris to think I am the be all and end all
Personalized as an individual throughout the galaxies.
Is there an eye that can peer through the universes
Discerning answers to my individual prayers?

My body will be mine to control, but not yours.
My athletic team will win this game, but not yours.
My country's political views will reign, but not yours.
My family will survive gunshots, but not yours.

Have faith in the unknown, they say.
Believe in the Father of Heaven who loves you.
I do have faith, and long for those comforting images,
And it is renewed at times.

By walks along the beach
Hikes in the forest
Scuba diving in the ocean
Watching stars at night.

I have faith that something is at the other end of
The Spyglass.

The Journey's End

For Alia Bergevin Morgan
October 24, 1971 - October 15, 2017

She, like some cancer patients, looked inward
Working through stages of dying
Denial, bargaining, depression
Wallowing at times in self-pity,
Shutting out family for long-past hurts
And railing against new medical understandings
As if that would have stopped aggressive cancer markers
From doubling behind her wall of pain.

But the reality slowly softened her realization.
That she and you and I will die no matter what.
How we choose to do it, is up to us.

She, like some cancer patients, began to look outward
How could she help the world see her, now?
What legacy could she leave others, now?
She volunteered, went to work and nurtured friends, now.
She set up *Alia and Angels* to help cancer families, now.

And then it began to happen, the slow transition
Of her psyche moving away from anger
Progressing, not to resignation and loss of hope,
But to acceptance and peace
And the right to die, pain-free, surrounded by love.

After the solemn viewing and funeral, fueled by faith,
A "Celebration of Life" to commemorate her spirit.
An intense day, a symphony of reverence.

On a beautiful, warm sunny autumn afternoon.
Music lilted above the river's quiet flowing.
Heartfelt testimonies were heard by family and friends
Who needed to talk and to listen and to reflect.
The gifts of the day embraced her spirit
With a bird release, full wingspan to freedom

People were vulnerable to her grace.
Their reverence and love for my daughter
Morphing over and over into thanksgiving
For a beautiful child, sister, wife, mother and friend.

Acknowledgements

Thanks to my long-time friend and artist, Ted Fusby, for the book cover "Somewhere Between" (2014).

"The Farm at Blende" was the winner for the Plainsong Poetry Contest. Published in The Final Note, Volume 4, 2012.

"Sharawadji: Graceful Disorder" with the painting by Jean Latka was printed in Road Trance, Southern Colorado Women's Poetry Series, Vol. IX, March 2009, p. 145.

"Hot Winds Blown Dry" was reprinted in February 2006, Volume 1, No. 12 http://centrifugaleye.com.

Quotes are from Margaret Wheatley, Leadership and the New Science, 1992.

Middle Creek Publishing Titles

Span
by David Anthony Martin

Deepening the Map
by David Anthony Martin

Phases
by Erika Moss Gordon

Cirque & Sky
by Kathleen Willard

Messiah Complex and Other Stories
by Michael Olin-Hitt

Lessons from Fighting The Black Snake at Standing Rock
by Nick Jaina and Leslie Orihel

Wild Be
by One Leaf

Bijoux
by David Anthony Martin

Sawhorse
by Tony Burfield

Almost Everything, Almost Nothing
by KB Ballentine

Across the Light
by Bruce Owens

Kimono Mountain
by Mike Parker

Somewhere Between
by Carol Fortino

www.ingramcontent.com/pod-product-compliance
Lightning Source LLC
Chambersburg PA
CBHW070100100426
42743CB00012B/2610